Quick and Easy Spelling, Reading and Writing Program
Book 5

Dictation Paragraph:

The Indian Boys' Night Out

bottom middle island trees friend

paddled heard layed canoe head sleep

One day there was a pond. At the bottom of the pond were two trees. In the middle of the pond were two islands. At the top of the were two teepees.

One night a little Indian boy went to his friend's teepee. They wanted to camp on the island. So they paddled their canoe to the first island. They made a fire. Then they heard noises, "Who, who, who!"

They got into their canoe and paddled to the second island. They made a fire. As soon as they layed their heads down to sleep they heard a noise, "Who, who, who!"

They jumped into their canoe and paddled home. Who made the noise? The owl.

Book 5 is a comprehensive collection of phonetic word families that includes sight words and paragraph dictation exercises. Writing Made Easy helps students with their writing skills.

Little Bug Adventure Books © 2009, 2011
www.littlebugadventures.com

Little Bug Adventure Books
Quick and Easy Spelling, Reading and Writing
Book 5

ISBN: 978-1-936288-18-2

copyright 2009, 2011
www.littlebugadventures.com

A division of Sand Prints Publishing Company.
Little Bug Adventures Books (USA)

Published in USA. Manufactured in USA by Sand Prints Publishing Co.

www.littlebugadventures.com

Sand Prints Publishing Company

Quick and Easy Spelling, Reading and Writing Program

Book 5

Quick and Easy Spelling and Grammar Book

Book 5

Objective: The student will learn words with same phonetic combinations. The student will learn sight words and word categories such as holidays. The student will learn phonetic rules such as double final consonant before adding ing. The student will learn grammar rules by writing dictation sentences. The student will learn how to write stories using Writing Made Easy.

Procedure:

1. Student learns words with same phonetic combinations.
2. Student learns spelling sight words and words in categories.
3. Student learns phonics rules. (double final consonant when adding ing)
4. Student learns grammar and phonetic rules while writing dictation sentences.
5. Student learns to write stories.

Outcome:

The student will master spelling words with same letter combinations. The student will master words in categories such as holidays. The student will master phonetic rules and grammar rules in dictation paragraphs. Student will learn to write stories.

Materials needed:

Quick and Easy Spelling and Grammar Book 5
Creative Writing Adventures Workbook 3
paper pencil

Quick and Easy Spelling and Grammar Program

Book 5

Book 5 introduces words with the same phonetic combinations. Spelling words are also taught in categories such as holidays, continents and oceans.

Book 5 is a comprehensive book that reinforces all sounds and grammar skills taught in Books 1-4 by writing dictation paragraphs. Book 5 teaches phonetic rules such as double the final consonant before adding er and est. It also teaches new grammar and capitalization rules in dictation paragraphs and stories.

Book 5 shows students the necessary components needed for writing a story by completing outlines and worksheets.

*** The purpose of always displaying spelling sight words is to allow the student to always see the word spelled correctly.

Quick and Easy Spelling, Reading and Writing Program

Pretest Spelling Test:
Begin using book where errors occur

Spelling Words

Book 1

1. cat
2. lip
3. rug
4. bed
5. mob
6. fix

Book 2

7. flat
8. drip
9. chug
10. sped
11. snob

Book 3

12. tramp
13. flask
14. string
15. drink

Book 4

16. scoping
17. fairies
18. wolves

Book 5

19. appointment
20. horticulture

Dictation Sentences:

Book 1

1. Can you mix the dip on the ship?

Book 2

2. Yes, Fred has two red sleds.

Book 3

3. Who handed the candy to the maid's son?

Book 4   **Pretest Spelling Dictation**
Dictation Paragraphs:

The Daisy Story

Grammar skills: , but to separate two compound sentences, change the y to i and add es, possessives

sight words: queen called Danny each pick loved special house

We have had many stories about fairies, but this fairy was a queen. She lived in house made of daisies so they called her Daisy. Daisy's son was named Danny. One Saturday morning in April Daisy picked forty-eight blackberries and made blackberry jam. All the fairies and Danny loved Daisy's special jam.

Book 5

Dictation Paragraph:

One Thanksgiving Day in Autumn

Grammar skills: possessives, ordinal numbers,
quotation marks, drop silent e before adding ing,
comma after yes or no
capitalization: months, holidays, names

Sight Words: cave bear everyone

On November the fourteenth, Bess's brother decided to take everyone fishing. Bess's friends wanted to go. John said, "No, we are going camping in the woods." That night they heard a noise coming from a cave. It was a bear hibernating for the winter.

Grammar Rules

1. Begin sentences with a capital letter. **T**he cat sat.
2. Begin names with a capital letter. **P**at
3. Begin holidays with a capital letter. **H**alloween
4. **Capitalize** the **first word** in **sentences** using **quotation marks.**   He said, "**C**ome here."
5. **Titles** and names begin with capital letters.
   Aunt Mary   **Mr.** Smith
6. Capitalize countries. **F**rance
7. Capitalize proper nouns, **L**ondon **B**ridge, **M**ain **S**treet
   months, **F**ebruary ; days of the week, **W**ednesday
8. Use , to **separate** objects in sequence.
   red**,** green**,** yellow and blue
9. Use commas to separate **appositives**.
   Bob**, the cop,** is here.
10. Use **commas** in dates. July 4**,** 1776
11. Use **commas** to separate city and states.
    Atlanta, Georgia
12. Use comma using **,and ,then** and **,but** to join **compound sentences.   ,and , but , then**
    We made lunch **, and** we are taking it to the park.
13. Use , after "**Yes**" and "**No**" at the beginning of a sentence. **Yes,   No,**
14. Use comma before **too** at the end of a sentence to mean **also**.   I want to go**, too**.

Grammar Rules

15. End sentences with a **.**, **?**, or **!**

16. Possessive: use **'s / s'** to show ownership.
    singular: Bob**'s** ship   Plural girl**s'** bikes

17. Use "**too**" to mean **too much**. **too** fast
    Use "**too**" to mean **also** at the end of a sentence.
    I want to go, **too**.

18. Use **an** before words that begin with a vowel. **an** <u>a</u>nt

19. Use **quotation marks** when people speak.
    He said, "Yes, I can go."

20. Use an **apostrophe** to replace missing letters in
    contractions.   can not   can't   does not   doesn't

21. Change **y** to **i** and add **es** to the end of words.
    fair<u>y</u> fair<u>ies</u>

22. Drop the **silent e** before adding **ing** to the end of
    words.   mak**e** mak**ing**

23. Add **es** to words ending in **x, ch, sh, s**.
    bo**x** bo**xes**, chur**ch** chur**ches**, di**sh** di**shes**,
    bu**s** bu**ses**

24. Change the **f** to **v** and add **es** to the end of words.
    wol**f** wol**ves**

25. Use **periods** in **abbreviations** and **titles**.
    Jan.   **Dr.**

25. **Double** the final consonant when adding
    ing / er / est   sit**ting** / hot**ter** / hot**test**

Quick and Easy Spelling, Reading and Writing Program
Book 5
Table of Contents

Sounds and Skills

Quick and Easy Spelling, Reading and Writing Program
Book 5
Table of Contents Continued

Table of Contents Continued

Silent Spelling Test

Numbers 1-20
10-100 by 10's
Ordinal numbers
Days
Months
Colors

Holidays
Relatives
Seasons
Continents
Oceans
Global terms

Silent Spelling Test

Numbers 1-10

1. one
2. two
3. three
4. four
5. five
6. six
7. seven
8. eight
9. nine
10. ten

Numbers 11-20

11. eleven
12. twelve
13. thirteen
14. fourteen
15. fifteen
16. sixteen
17. seventeen
18. eighteen
19. nineteen
20. twenty

10 – 100 by 10's
Th, M, B

10	ten
20	twenty
30	thirty
40	**forty**
50	fifty
60	sixty
70	seventy
80	eighty
90	ninety
100	hundred
1000	thousand
1,000,000	million
1,000,000,000	billion

Ordinal Numbers
1st-20th

1st first	11th eleventh
2nd second	12th twelfth
3rd third	13th thirteenth
4th fourth	14th fourteenth
5th fifth	15th fifteenth
6th sixth	16th sixteenth
7th seventh	17th seventeenth
8th eighth	18th eighteenth
9th **ninth**	19th nineteenth
10th tenth	20th **twentieth**

Silent Spelling Test

Relatives

mother
father
son
daughter
brother
sister
grandmother
grandfather
aunt
uncle
nephew
niece
cousin

Continents

North America
South America
Europe
Asia
Africa
Australia
Antarctica

Oceans

Atlantic Ocean
Pacific Ocean
Indian Ocean
Arctic Ocean

Global Terms

longitude
latitude
equator
North Pole
South Pole
Prime Meridian
Arctic Circle
Antarctic Circle

Seasons

fall
winter
spring
summer

Silent Spelling Test

Days of the Week

Sunday
Monday
Tuesday
Wednesday
Thursday
Friday
Saturday

Color Words

red
blue
yellow
green
purple
brown
black
white

Holidays

New Year's Eve / New Year's Day
Valentine's Day
St. Patrick's Day
Easter
Mother's Day
Father's Day
Fourth of July
No Holiday
Labor Day
Halloween
Thanksgiving Day
Christmas Eve / Christmas Day

Months of the Year

January
February
March
April
May
June
July
August
September
October
November
December

Silent Spelling Test

Write in **words** the following categories in order.

1. Numbers 1-10
2. Numbers 10-20
3. Numbers by 10-100, Th, M, B
4. Ordinal numbers 1st-20th
5. Days of the Week
6. Colors (8)
7. Months of the Year
8. Holidays (one for every month except August)
9. Relatives (13)
10. Continents
11. Oceans
12. Global Terms (8)
13. Seasons

Silent Spelling Test

Numbers 1-10

1. one
2. two
3. three
4. four
5. five
6. six
7. seven
8. eight
9. nine
10. ten

Numbers 11-20

11. eleven
12. twelve
13. thirteen
14. fourteen
15. fifteen
16. sixteen
17. seventeen
18. eighteen
19. nineteen
20. twenty

10 – 100 by 10's
Th, M, B

10	ten
20	twenty
30	thirty
40	**forty**
50	fifty
60	sixty
70	seventy
80	eighty
90	ninety
100	hundred
1000	thousand
1,000,000	million
1,000,000,000	billion

Ordinal Numbers
1st-20th

1st first	11th eleventh
2nd second	12th tw**elf**th
3rd third	13th thirteenth
4th fourth	14th fourteenth
5th fifth	15th fifteenth
6th sixth	16th sixteenth
7th seventh	17th seventeenth
8th eighth	18th eighteenth
9th **ninth**	19th nineteenth
10th tenth	20th **twentieth**

Silent Spelling Test

Days of the Week

Sunday
Monday
Tuesday
Wednesday
Thursday
Friday
Saturday

Color Words

red
blue
yellow
green
purple
brown
black
white

Holidays

New Year's Eve / New Year's Day
Valentine's Day
St. Patrick's Day
Easter
Mother's Day
Father's Day
Fourth of July
No Holiday
Labor Day
Halloween
Thanksgiving Day
Christmas Eve / Christmas Day

Months of the Year

January
February
March
April
May
June
July
August
September
October
November
December

Silent Spelling Test

Relatives

mother
father
son
daughter
brother
sister
grandmother
grandfather
aunt
uncle
nephew
niece
cousin

Global Terms

longitude
latitude
equator
North Pole
South Pole
Prime Meridian
Arctic Circle
Antarctic Circle

Seasons

fall
winter
spring
summer

Continents

North America
South America
Europe
Asia
Africa
Australia
Antarctica

Oceans

Atlantic Ocean
Pacific Ocean
Indian Ocean
Arctic Ocean

Book 5

Spelling

Using Letter Combinations & Grammar Skills

ble Spelling Words

table
rumble
tumble
cable
fable
ramble
sample
simple
handle
ladle
paddle
little
rattle
wobble
castle

Dictation Sentences:

Grammar skills: contractions, **,** to separate two
compound sentences

1. The eight boys paddled their little canoe down the dark river.
2. I can hear the rumbling coming nearer to me.
3. Hold the handle, so the bike won't wobble.

ight Spelling Words

fight   **Sight Word:**
light
might   off
right
sight
tight
slight
fright

Add en		**Add ed**
tight	tighten	tightened
fright	frighten	frightened

Dictation Sentences:

Grammar skills: comma to separate two compound sentences

1. Was the brave Indian frightened when the light went out?
2. He was right. There was a fight.
3. The girl tightened the jar, so the top won't come off.

Add ly to these words

love

_____

careful

_____

quiet

_____

nice

_____

sweet

_____

loud

_____

proud

_____

quick

_____

soft

_____

Opposites	/	Antonyms	/	Synonyms for antonyms
happy		unhappy		sad
tidy		untidy		messy
well		unwell		ill
kind		unkind		mean
light		heavy		
laugh		cry		
clean		dirty		
rough		smooth		
sharp		blunt		
long		short		
lost		found		

Dictation Paragraph:

The Chinese Story

Grammar skills: opposites, numbers, quotation marks
Capitalization: days of the week, countries, cities

Sight Words: because people Shiam every kind village

Once upon a time a little boy lived with his mother in China. He was an unhappy little boy because the people in the village were hungry. He lived in a small village called Shiam. Every Monday, Wednesday, and Friday he went with his mother to the village to look for food. He found a bag under a black stone. There were six thousand, four hundred and forty-five pieces of gold in the bag. He used the gold to buy food for the people in the village. The people said, "Thank you very much! You are very kind."

Add er and est Practice

tall	taller	tallest
new	newer	newest
high	higher	highest
neat	neater	neatest
warm	warmer	warmest
old	older	oldest
sharp	sharper	sharpest
smooth	smoother	smoothest

---

fine	finer	finest
nice	nicer	nicest
ripe	riper	ripest
tame	tamer	tamest
wise	wiser	wisest
pale	paler	palest
large	larger	largest

Soft g and c Spelling Words

g	c
giant	city
gem	bicycle
gym	tricycle
digest	center
page	cell
huge	cyclone
ginger	fancy
danger	ice
magic	excited
	decided

Dictation Paragraph:

The Fancy Tricycle

Grammar skills: Soft g and c, ed past tense, quotation marks
Capitalization: holidays

Sight Words: once upon invented dreamed brought tricycle magic excited window snowing back

Once upon a time when the tricycle was first invented, a little girl dreamed that one day she would have one. Santa Claus heard her wish and brought her a purple tricycle. This tricycle was magic. It could talk. On Christmas morning it said, "Come here. Would you like a ride?"

Daisy was so excited she ran to the window and saw it was snowing. She ran to the tricycle. Her mother called, "Come back."

The tricycle said, "No, we are going to the North Pole."

Mr. Brown's Dog
Review Story
Dictation Paragraph

Grammar skills: possessives, numbers, drop silent e when adding ing, colors, change y to i when adding es

Capital letters: months, days, titles (Mr.), names

Sight Words: bicycle dog

In August we went to Mr. Brown's house on Tuesday, Wednesday, and Thursday. We liked riding our bicycle over to Mr. Brown's house. Mr. Brown said, "Come in." Mr. Brown's dog had seven black and white puppies. When we counted the spots on all the puppies there were eight thousand, five hundred and forty-three spots.

Doubling the final consonant
before adding ing

tip	tipping
dip	dipping
rip	ripping
drip	dripping
flip	flipping
hop	hopping
hit	hitting
bat	batting
skip	skipping
slip	slipping
run	running
shut	shutting
shop	shopping
cut	cutting
sit	sitting
stop	stopping
tug	tugging
spin	spinning
trot	trotting
pet	petting
put	putting
rub	rubbing

Doubling the final consonant before adding ing

tip   _____

dip   _____

rip   _____

drip   _____

flip   _____

hop   _____

hit   _____

bat   _____

skip   _____

slip   _____

run   _____

shut   _____

shop   _____

cut   _____

sit   _____

stop   _____

tug   _____

spin   _____

trot   _____

pet   _____

put   _____

rub   _____

Never Pet a Bat

Dictation Paragraph

Grammar skills: double final consonant before adding ing

Sight Words: decided rain idea cage

One day Jan decided to go shopping for a pet. She began running to the pet shop because it was dripping raindrops. As she went skipping into the shop, she saw a bat rubbing his wings.

Jan decided taking the bat home would be a good idea. When she was putting the bat into the cage it started biting her and tugging on her arm. The clerk saw the bat hopping around and began hitting the bat. Jan went home without a bat for a pet.

Draw on board as the story is read.

Dictation Story:

The Indian Boys' Night Out

Sight Words: bottom middle island trees friend

paddled layed canoe head sleep teepees fire

One day there was a pond. At the bottom of the pond were two trees. In the middle of the pond were two islands. At the top of the pond were two teepees.

One night a little Indian boy went to his friend's teepee. They wanted to camp on the island. So they paddled their canoe to the first island. They made a fire. Then they heard noises, "Who, who, who!"

They got into their canoe and paddled to the second island. They made a fire. As soon as they layed their heads down to sleep they heard a noise, "Who, who, who!"

They jumped into their canoe and paddled home. Who made the noise? **An owl.**

Compound Spelling Words

flashlight	livingroom	rooftop	bedroom
treehouse	carseat	lighthouse	snowflake
dustpan	backyard	truckstop	boathouse
raindrop	highway	notebook	windshield
billboard	stationwagon	headlight	hotdog
doghouse	superman	doorway	windsurf
fireplace	firelight	livingroom	

Dictation Paragraph:

The Treehouse

Grammar skills: compound words, possessives their, there

Sight Words: above soon large use write

Once two boys camped out in a treehouse above their dog's doghouse in their backyard. There was a livingroom and bedroom in their treehouse. They brought a flashlight and a notebook to their house. Soon it began to rain large raindrops on the rooftop. They had to use their flashlight to write in their notebook.

Dictation Paragraph:

The State Fair

Grammar skills: commas in sequence, possessives, capitals, doubling, final consonants, colors
Capitalization: holidays, names, proper nouns, states

Sight Words: turkey Ohio State Fair prize wonderful feathers

Once upon a time there was a turkey farm in Ohio. It was Thanksgiving Day and millions of people wanted to buy turkeys. Mr. Brown's turkeys were the biggest turkeys in Ohio. At the Ohio State Fair, Mr. Brown's turkey won first prize because of his wonderful tail feathers of red, yellow, blue, orange, purple, and green.

Double the final consonant and add ing and ed Spelling Words

stop	stopped	stopping
hop	hopped	hopping
skip	skipped	skipping
zip	zipped	zipping
flip	flipped	flipping
jab	jabbed	jabbing
chat	chatted	chatting
pet	petted	petting
rub	rubbed	rubbing
rip	ripped	ripping

Dictation Paragraph:

The Active Pet Shop

Grammar skills: double the final consonant and add ed and ing, quotation marks, change y to i - add es, Capitalization: months, names, days

One summer day John decided to visit a pet shop. It was a busy Saturday in August. John loved petting all the animals. He also liked watching the animals hopping and skipping about.

Once he petted a rabbit, and the rabbit rubbed his nose on his hand. John said, "You are a nice little rabbit. I want to take you home." Now John has six black and white bunnies because the rabbit had babies.

Add es to words ending in x, ch, sh, s
Spelling Words

bush	bushes	torch	torches
watch	watches	glass	glasses
coach	coaches	bus	buses
brush	brushes	match	matches
box	boxes	church	churches
fox	foxes	dish	dishes
peach	peaches		

Dictation Paragraph:

A Church Picnic

Grammar skills: double final consonant and add ing,
add es to sh, x, ch and sh, quotation marks,
change f to v and add es.

sight words: afternoon, invite brought, light, watched, preacher

One Sunday afternoon the church wives decided to invite other churches to a picnic. Coaches and buses brought many people to the picnic. People brought dishes and glasses in boxes for the people to use. Two foxes watched the picnic behind some bushes.   It was getting dark so the wives used matches to light torches. The preacher said, "Everyone is having fun."

eigh Spelling Words

eight	ate
sleigh	
weigh	way
weight	
reindeer	

Dictation Paragraph:

Eight Reindeer

Grammar skills: proper noun

Sight Words: hay which

Once upon a time there were eight reindeer who lived at the North Pole. One day they ate so much hay they decided to weigh to see which reindeer weighed the most. On their way to the barn, Santa told the reindeer to take him for a ride on his sleigh. They did not get to weigh.

Change y to i and add er Spelling Words

busy	busier
early	earlier
hungry	hungrier
heavy	heavier
happy	happier
shiny	shinier
slippy	slippier

Dictation Paragraph:

The Happy Little Birds

Sight Words: little loved work woke

Once upon a time there were eight, happy little birds. They loved to work. They found out that the earlier they woke up, the hungrier they got. As they worked, they found that the heavier the weights, the slippier they became. But as the day went on, they found that the busier they were, the happier they became.

ie says e Spelling Words

ie words

chief	niece
relief	piece
belief	believe
shield	achieve
yield	grief
field	

Dictation Sentences and Paragraph:

Grammar skills: proper nouns

Sight Words: great money year deal wonderful

1. The chief said, "The field has yielded a great crop of corn."
2. It was a relief to the Indians.
3. They received money for their crop.

The Indian Chief

The Indian chief said, "The field has yielded a wonderful crop of corn this year." This was a great relief to the Indians. They received a great deal of money for their wonderful crop.

Ordinal Numbers Spelling Words

first	eleventh
second	twelfth
third	thirteenth
fourth	fourteenth
fifth	fifteenth
sixth	sixteenth
seventh	seventeenth
eighth	eighteenth
ninth	nineteenth
tenth	twentieth

Dictation Paragraph:

Horseback Riding Contest

Grammar skills: commas in a series, possessives

Sight Words: month each Atlanta prizes awarded children group

On the first, second, and third day of each month, Atlanta has a horseback riding contest. In August the prizes are awarded to the first, second, third, fourth, fifth, and sixth best riders. In the children's group there is a prize for the twentieth best rider.

Change the y to i and add es and ed Spelling Words

try	tries	tried
cry	cries	cried
hurry	hurries	hurried
deny	denies	denied
pry	pries	pried
fry	fries	fried

Dictation Paragraph:

The Flying Boy

Grammar skills: doubled final consonant and add ed,
change y to i and add es and ed
capitalization: days, names

Sight Words: garage door climbed roof

One Wednesday morning John tried to fly. He pried open the garage door and climbed on the roof. He hurried and flapped his arms. He fell to the ground and cried. He denied that he tried to fly.

Double the final consonant, add er and est
Spelling Words

wet	wetter	wettest
happy	happier	happiest
hot	hotter	hottest
slippy	slippier	slippiest
sad	sadder	saddest
red	redder	reddest

Dictation Paragraphs:

The Wettest Day of the Year

Grammar skills: doubled final consonant and add er and est
its it's, either, quotation marks, appositive, contractions, possessives
capitalization: oceans, months, names

**Sight Words: exclaimed least Luke board away
current really either**

On August the eighteenth, the wettest day of the year, Skipper decided to windsurf in the Atlantic Ocean. "This is not my happiest day," Skipper exclaimed.

"At least it's hotter than last year, " said his friend, Luke. "I nearly froze."

As they talked Luke's board slipped away from him. The board lost its way in the current. Luke said, "It really isn't my happiest day, either."

Dictation Paragraphs:

Halloween on a Dark Night

Grammar skills: quotation marks, exclamation marks, double final
consonant and add ed, their, there

Sight Words: rainy play trick took front path

One dark, rainy Halloween night three boys decided to play a trick on
a friend. They took his pumpkin off his front porch. As they ran down a
path they met a goblin. The goblin said, "Give me your pumpkin!"
There was a scrambling of little feet. The boys dropped the pumpkin
and ran all the way home. The goblin was really their friend. He took his
pumpkin back home.

Please Ask for the Peas

Grammar skills: titles, appositives, quotation marks, their
capitalization: names. titles

Sight Words: dinner served family refused vine Williams everyone
telephone room grow thicker reached castle full envy Queen

One night at the dinner table Dr. Williams served peas to his family.
His daughter, Penny, refused to eat the peas. She said, "No way, Jose!"
Dr. Williams heard the telephone ringing. When he left the room Penny
threw the peas out the window. A vine began to grow over the house. It
became thicker and thicker until it reached the sky. Penny climbed the
vine and found a pea castle full of peas. The pea people made her their
Pea Queen. Everyone was pea green with envy.

The moral of the story is, Don't eat your peas.

tion Spelling Words

	Scientific Terms
potion	
carnation	
nation	fertilization
lotion	sanitation
caption	pollination
fiction	respiration
vacation	hibernation
decoration	elevation
complication	polarization
invitation	navigation
locomotion	gravitation
capitalization	motion
action	invention
sensation	operation
generation	reaction
subtraction	contraction
fraction	relation
imagination	elevation
	inflation

Dictation Paragraph:

The Vacation

Grammar skills: contractions, there, their, they're, too, to, two, possessives

Sight Words: summer late home parents

Late one summer night there were eight boys who decided to go on a vacation. They got information about their vacation from the station. They didn't want to plan their destination too far from home. They had a notion that their parents might have a reaction to their plans. One of the boy's relations heard about their vacation and told their parents. Two parents didn't like the plans for a vacation and the notion became fiction. The boys said that they were only using their imagination.

apartment	ferment
department	moment
compartment	employment
development	enjoyment
arrangement	ointment
cement	appointment
government	advertisement
comment	compliment
element	

Dictation Paragraph:

The Queen's New Apartment

Grammar skills: root words, possessives capitalization: months

Sight Words: develop ordered arranged project finished

Once upon a time a queen decided to develop a new apartment complex. Her government arranged the development near her apartment. After all the arrangements were made, cement was ordered. The department arranged to have the project finished by late October.

ure Spelling Words

structure
lecture
nature
mature
future
culture
horticulture
pasture
rupture
texture

vulture
temperature
adventure
capture
agriculture
cure
pure
sure

Dictation Paragraph:

A Lecture on Vultures

Grammar skills: it's, its, possessives
capitalization: proper names, countries

**Sight Words: during living drew studied eggs
Boston Museum of Science display student**

During a lecture on temperature and its relationship to vultures living in nature, a student drew a picture of a family of vultures. The lecturer discussed his adventure to Africa where he studied vultures. He studied the structure of the bird's nest. Dr. Williams decided it's time to capture a vulture. He climbed the highest mountain. He found three of the vulture's eggs. Now they are on display in the Boston Museum of Science.

Vultures in Africa
Dictation Paragraph

Grammar skills: double final consonant before adding est, quotation marks, possessives
capitalization: proper names, countries, I

Sight Words: broken climbed
Dallas Museum of Science

One night I dreamed about an adventure to Africa where I studied vultures. I climbed the highest mountain on the wettest day in November. I took a picture of a vulture's nest. I said, "Look, the vulture has babies." I took one of the vulture's broken eggs back to the Dallas Museum of Science.

ary Spelling Words

January
February
canary
rudimentary - not advanced or developed
mortuary - of death or burial
commentary - comment
dictionary
secondary - not first
contrary
constabulary - police force
secretary
diary - daily record
legendary - famous or existing in a legend
stationary - not moving
Mary
military - having to do with the armed forces
primary - first, beginning
visionary - can see visions
solitary - alone
sedimentary - matter that settles at the bottom of a liquid
temporary - for a short time
veterinary - the treatment of animals

A Temporary Secretary
ary Spelling Words

Grammar skills: quotation marks
capitalization: proper names, months

**Sight Words: arrived California Military Base
soldier asked How long answered
served World War II**

One winter day in February a new secretary arrived at a California Military Base with her dictionary. On her first day she was told to write a commentary on the solitary soldier. The secretary asked, "How long do I have to write the commentary?"

The captain answered, "You have one month to find a legendary soldier." The secretary found a hero who had served in World War II.

A Legendary Day in February
Dictation Paragraph

Grammar skills: quotation marks, contractions
capitalization: proper names, days, months

Sight Words: **writing   anywhere   recent   parade
officer   Purple Heart Medal   bravery**

One day a temporary secretary was writing in her diary. She couldn't find her dictionary anywhere. She wanted to write a commentary on her recent vacation. On Wednesday afternoon, she saw a military parade at the mortuary. An officer was awarded the Purple Heart Medal for bravery. The secretary said, "This is a legendary day in February."

aw Spelling Words

draw	awkward
hawk	paw
law	saw
lawyer	raw
straw	lawn
awful	fawn
squawk	shawl
crawl	claw

Dictation Paragraphs:

The Hawk and the Fawn

Grammar skills: there, their, change y to i and add es
capitalization: names

Sight Words: Harry named below next while watched

Once upon a time there was a hawk named Harry. His best friend was a fawn named Misty. Harry found some straw in the lawn and made a nest in a tree. Misty found some leaves on the ground and made a bed below Harry's nest.

One morning they heard a squawk in the next tree. "They're eight baby owls in a nest," said Harry. Their mother had left, and one of the babies had hurt its claw. Harry went to see the babies and helped the little owls while Misty watched from below. Their mother came back, and Harry went home.

au Spelling Words

haul
auto
Paul
author
laundry
faucet
because
naughty
daughter
caught
August
vault
fault

Dictation Paragraph:

Paul in the Laundromat
Grammar skills: au words, possessives, a, an
capitalization: names, months, cities, proper nouns

Sight Words: owned front money raced away laundromat

Once there was a man named Paul who owned a laundromat in Boston. His daughter, Shawn, was an author and sometimes helped her father at the laundromat.

One day in August Shawn saw an auto park in front of the bank. A naughty man went inside the bank and robbed the vault. He hauled money to his auto and raced away because he didn't want to get caught. A cop saw the robber and caught the naughty man. The robber said, "It's not my fault."

all and al Spelling Words

all words	al words	al words (ending)
recall	always	functional
small	already	instrumental
ball	malt	constitutional
snowball	chalk	departmental
hall	walk	developmental
install	stalk	mental
rainfall	talk	musical
waterfall	Walter	spiritual
stall	conventional	
wall	vocal	
call		
mall		
tall		

Dictation Paragraph:

The Snowball Fight

Grammar skills: a, an, compound words

Sight Words: changed throw built behind

Once a boy decided to have a snowball fight near an icy waterfall. The rainfall had changed to snow so they began to throw small snowballs at each other. They built a snowman near a tall wall behind the mall. They named him Frosty.

ought Spelling Words

bought
thought
fought
ought
brought
sought

Dictation Paragraph:

The Kangaroo

Grammar skills: ought words, commas in series, change y to i add es, capitalization: names

Sight Words: market peaches pears flowers price cost

One day a kangaroo named Joey thought he should go to the market. He wanted to buy peaches, pears, and plums. He brought a bag with him. On the way he bought some flowers from some ladies. He fought with the ladies over the price of the flowers. He thought they ought to cost less.

ie and ei says e Spelling Words

piece
niece
grief
believe
achieve

i before e except after c

receive
ceiling
receipt

Dictation Paragraph:

The Tornado

Grammar skills: ordinal numbers, possessives, **ie** says **e**, **ie** before **e** except after **c**, capitalization: months, names

Sight Words: sharing tornado gone through

On the twelfth of August Jennifer's niece received a box from the post office. She couldn't believe she received a piece of her aunt's ceiling. It was her aunt's way of sharing her grief about the tornado that had gone through her house.

ie says i Spelling Words

pie
cried
flies
died
lies

Dictation Paragraphs:

The Pies

Grammar skills: exclamation marks, contractions, quotation marks, change **y** to **i** and add **es**

Sight Words: Many papers eat

Many flies were around some pies in a window. The ladies making the pies cried, "Go away, flies!"

Many of the flies died as the ladies began to hit the flies with some papers. The ladies cried, "Now all the flies have died, and they can't eat our pies."

ei says a Spelling Words Review

eight
eighteen
eighty
freight
weigh
weight
neighbor
Cleigh

Dictation Paragraph:

Eight New Puppies

Grammar skills: ei says a, change y to i add es,
ordinal numbers, possessives
capitalization: streets, names, months

Sight Words: together large

On the eighteenth day of May, Cleigh decided to go
to his neighbor's house at eighty North Freight Street. He
wanted to weigh his eight new puppies. The puppies were
large and weighed seventy pounds all together.

Prefixes

pre means before

prewar
precooked

in means not

incorrect
inactive

dis means not

dishonest
disbelief

mis means wrongly

misued
misplaced
mislead

re means again

reuse
reread
rejoining
repaying
repeated
recheck
replace

un means not

unknown
uncertain
unlikely
unlock
unzip
unbutton

Suffixes

	Syllables		Rootword
weakness	weak ness		weak
kindness	kind ness		kind
darkness	dark ness		dark
wetness	wet ness		wet
helpful	help ful		help
tearful	tear ful		tear
hopeful	hope ful		hope
restless	rest less		rest
careless	care less		care
bookless	book less		book
shoeless	shoe less		shoe
fearless	fear less		fear
helpless	help less		help
teacher	teach er		teach
climber	climb er		climb
owner	own er		own
walker	walk er		walk
talker	talk er		talk
helper	help er		help

Possessives Review

Singular	Plural
the girl's cat	those girls' cats
a dog's house	those dogs' houses
a cat's pillow	those cats' pillows
a horse's stall	those horses' stalls
the child's play	those children's play
a man's chair	those men's chairs
the clerk's money	those clerks' money
a fish's bowl	those fishes' bowls
a fox's den	those foxes' dens
a cloud's lining	those clouds' lining
a woman's cup	those women's cups
a bear's cub	those bears' cups
a snake's cage	those snakes' cages
John's hat	

Dictation Paragraph:

Bess's Wettest Day of the Year

Grammar skills: possessives, double final consonant before adding **est**
ordinal numbers, change the **y** to **i** and add **est**
capitalization: months, names

Sight Words: restless rode

On August the nineteenth, the wettest day of the year, Bess decided to ride her bike. The other girls' bikes were at home, but Bess was restless. She was the happiest when she rode her bike.

Dictation Paragraphs:

One Thanksgiving Day in Autumn

Grammar skills: possessives, ordinal numbers, quotation marks, drop silent **e** before adding **ing**, comma after yes or no
capitalization: months, holidays, names

Sight Words: cave bear everyone

On November the fourteenth, Bess's brother decided to take everyone fishing. Bess's friends wanted to go. John said, "No, we are going camping in the woods." That night they heard a noise coming from a cave. It was a bear hibernating for the winter.

Dictation Paragraph:

The Baby Bird in the Nest

Grammar skills: possessives,
change the **y** to **i** and add **est** and **es**

Sight Words: foot return

One day a boy went into the woods and saw the prettiest bird. She had babies in her nest. One baby fell out of the nest and landed near the boy's foot. The baby's wing was hurt. The boy helped the baby bird return to her nest.

Dictation Paragraphs:

Santa Claus in the North Pole

Grammar skills: possessives, compound words, quotation marks
capitalization: days, titles

Sight Words: good   school   together

Last Saturday night Mr. and Mrs. Claus were sitting by their cozy fireplace. Santa Claus said, "Mrs. Smith's girls and boys have been very good this year."

Mrs. Claus said, "Yes, why don't we give them a party?"

All the elves got together and made decorations. The party was at school. Everyone had fun.

The Girl's Cat

Grammar skills: plural possessives, there, their,
drop final **e** when adding **ing**
capitalization: days, names

Sight Words: scare pillow woken several different

One day Bess's cat was lying down on her favorite pillow when she was woken by several girls riding their bikes. The girls' bikes were very noisy. The girls' voices were very loud. Bess's cat decided to scare the girls. She walked to a brick wall where the girls' bikes were parked. When the girls came to get on their bikes, Bess's cat jumped on their heads and scared them. The girls picked a different street to ride their bikes the next Saturday.

ew Spelling Words

new
knew
flew
grew
dew
crew
stew

Dictation Paragraph:

The Army Crew

Grammar skills: ew words, change f to v and add es
change **y** to **i** and add **es**, homonyms,
drop silent **e** when adding **ing**, there, their,
compound words

Sight Words: cook able smell put gave shiny glow

One day an Army crew went to a new island, where no one lived, to cook stew. The crew knew no one would be able to smell their stew. There were herbs that grew on the island that the crew put into their stew. As it grew dark dew formed on the leaves of the herbs which gave a shiny glow. Fireflies flew near the stew, and the crew could eat their stew by the firefly light.

Homophones Spelling Words

one	won	
by	buy	
tale	tail	
made	maid	
new	knew	
our	hour	
no	know	
weak	week	
for	four	
blue	blew	
pair	pear	
hair	hare	
son	sun	
to	two	too
their	there	they're

Dictation Paragraph:

Hurricane Street

Grammar skills: homophones, possessives, contractions
capitalization: streets, names

**Sight Words: Wendy witch ate Hurricane Street
another broom recovered**

Once upon a time there was a witch named Wendy who ate eight black apples from Hurricane Street. She would weigh her apples on the way to the market which was near her home.

One day another witch wanted the witch's apples. She stole Wendy's apples when she wasn't looking. The bad witch ran all the way down the street. Wendy got on her broom and recovered the apples. Now there are no more bad witches on Hurricane Street.

Dictation Paragraph:

Skipper's Surfing Adventure

Grammar skills: quotation marks, exclamation marks, to, too, two, double final consonant, add er and ing

Sight Words: surfing choppy waves high huge knocked after finally Shorewatch team rescue why today weak answer

One day Skipper decided to go surfing. The water was choppy. The waves were too high. A huge wave knocked Skipper off his board. After spinning around in the wave, Skipper finally yelled, "Help!"

Two members of the Shorewatch team came to rescue Skipper. They said, "Why did you decide to surf today?" Skipper was too weak to answer.

Dictation Paragraphs:

A Turkey Day in Tennessee

Grammar skills: commas, titles, possessives, appositive, contractions, ordinal numbers, double final consonant before adding ed, change f to v and add es; capitalization: months, days, titles, names

Sight Words: favorite changing colors crown wrote story adventure

On November sixteenth, Mr. Brown decided to sell all his turkeys. Mr. Brown's favorite turkey was Big Red. Big Red's tail had red, blue, yellow, and green feathers. Mr. Brown couldn't sell Big Red. He sent Big Red to Mr. Smith's farm.

Mrs. Smith's son, Billy, played with Big Red and took him for long walks in the woods. It was fall and the leaves were changing colors. One leaf fell on Big Red's head. It looked like a king's crown.

Just then, Billy saw a wolf behind a tree. Several wolves popped their heads out from behind the trees. Billy and Big Red ran all the way back to Mr. Smith's farm. On Saturday a reporter wrote a story about Big Red's adventure.

Dictation Story: **A Sick Boy on a Mountain**

Sight Words: journey special earlier halfway worrying whole mountain complained discussions engineers designed coasters demonstrated different kitchen operated controls cell anything

It was Christmas Eve at the North Pole. Mr. and Mrs. Santa Claus and all the elves were busily gathering toys for their midnight journey. This was a very special Christmas Eve. Santa was leaving earlier than usual this year. He needed to drive his sleigh halfway around the world to deliver a present to a very brave little boy. Santa wanted to give the present to the little boy before he went to sleep. Santa and the elves had been worrying about little Billy for a whole year. Little Billy had been sick in bed on top of a mountain all year. He was so brave and never cried or complained at all.

The elves wanted to give Billy the best present they ever made. After many late night discussions the engineers said they knew how to make the best present. The chief engineer said, "We can make a super train."

Now this train was like no other train. The engineers designed a train with tracks that hung from the ceiling and went all over the house. Eight different trains ran on different tracks. Some were like roller coasters that ran at high speeds. A computer at Billy's bed operated all the controls. He had train tracks that ran to the kitchen and all over the house. His mother put his lunch on a train. His father put his tools on a train. All he had to do was call on his cell phone and anything could be delivered by train.

Billy had been all alone on top of his mountain, but when people found out about his wonderful trains, they came from everywhere to see them. Billy learned how to fix his trains from the tool kit given to him by the elves. He became one of the best train engineers in the country and wrote several books about trains. He demonstrated his different trains on the internet. Many children in hospitals around the world bought his trains and loved them. Billy was on television with his own train show. He became famous.

Dictation Letter:

Grammar skills: change the i and add es
capitalization: days, salutations

Sight Words: Sincerely kangaroo zoo keeper

Kangaroos in the Zoo

Dear Zoo Keeper,

We heard there is a new kangaroo in your zoo. It carries two babies in its pouch. We would like to come see your kangaroos on Saturday, February 9th.

Sincerely,

Mrs. Smith's class

ial Spelling Words

commercial
financial
confidential
essential
partial
credentials

Dictation Paragraph:

The Commercial

Sight Words: advisor sponsor company checked

Once a financial advisor decided to sponsor a commercial for his company. He wanted a partial slot on a television station. It was essential that this remain confidential until they checked his credentials.

ian Spelling Words

musician
physician
politician
Venetian
historian
librarian
custodian
comedian

Dictation Paragraph:

Grammar Skills: use commas in sequence
capitalization: proper noun

Sight Words: included wife busy

The Venetian

Once there was a Venetian man who had many professions. Some of his jobs included being a musician, physician, politician, historian, comedian and custodian. His wife was a librarian. He was a busy man.

ious Spelling Words

suspicious - questionable
ferocious - scary
delicious - tastes great
facetious - humorous, witty
nutritious - food good for you
cautious - careful
atrocious - outrageous, shocking
malicious - spiteful, evil
suspicious - doubtful
voracious - excessively greedy,
vicarious - suffered or done in place of another

Dictation Paragraph:

Grammar skills: double the final consonant adding ed

Sight Words: family crept close creeping

The Ferocious Tiger

Everyone became cautious when a ferocious tiger was spotted near the forest. As a family ate their delicious lunch, the malicious tiger crept close to their table. They heard a suspicious noise and saw the atrocious animal creeping nearer. They grabbed their nutritious lunch and ran inside.

Dictation Paragraphs:

The Fairies Dance

Grammar skills: they're, there, their, ordinal numbers change f to v and add es, drop silent e before adding ing

Sight Words: whispered snickered inquired

Once upon a time there were elves watching twelve fairies dancing. "They're dancing in a circle," whispered the first elf.

"They're holding hands," added the second elf.

"They're jumping all around," snickered the third elf.

"Do you see their wings are shining in the moonlight?" inquired the fourth elf.

After finishing their dance, mushrooms grew in a circle just where the fairies had performed their dance.

Body Parts Spelling Words

head
shoulder
waist
arm
hands
hair
eyes
ears
nose
chin
mouth
neck
chest
fingers
hips
thigh
knee
toes
fingernails
elbow
foot

Geometry Spelling Words

parallel lines
intercepting lines
square
triangle
parallelogram rectangle
right angle
acute angle
obtuse angle
perimeter - the distance around a figure
area

Solids/Volume Spelling Words

Solids
cube
cuboid
cylinder
sphere

Mass
kilograms
grams
1kg=1000g

Capacity
liters

Length
centimeters cm
meters   m
kilometers   km

Index

Book 5 Spelling Sight Words

A

able
above
adventure
advisor
after
also
animals
another
answered
anything
anywhere
arranged
arrived
asked
ate
Atlanta
Atlantic Ocean
awarded
away

B

brave
biggest
became
board
bravery
below
built
Boston Museum
of Science
brick
busy
broken
because
back
brought
bicycle
bottom
broom

C

California
cage
canoe
case
children
climbed
cost
cook
changing
colors
castle

Book 5 Spelling Sight Words

D
door
develop
display
different
discussions
deliver
drew
Dallas
during
display
designed
demonstrated
dreamed
dog
deal
dinner
decided

E
every
exclaimed
either
eggs
everyone
engineer
excited
envy
eat
earlier
each

F
food
favorite
first
feather
friend
froze
front
from
foot
favorite
fireflies
flew
fire
field
family
finished
flowers

G
good
group
garage
give
gone
glow
great
grow
gave

H
hold
hungry
hay
highest
hero
head
Hurricane
horses
how
Harry
huge
home
high
halfway

I
Indian
invented
idea
icy
island
its
it's
included
inquired
invented
idea

J
journey

K
kind
knocked
kitchen

L
look
Luke
late
less
lying
least
layed
large
long
little
living

M
money
might
mountain
market
mushroom
magic
month
middle

N
nice
New York
next
named

Book 5 Spelling Sight Words

O

open
Ohio State Fair
off
only
office
ordered
operated
once
other
officer

P

presents
Pole
prize
parents
projects
price
papers
pillow
picked
paddled
play
path
parade
put
Peaches
Pears
Purple Heart
price

Q

Queen

R

roof
really
rainy
refused
recovered
recent
restless
rode
return
rescue

S

Shiam
showing
sleep
soon
screamed
served
studied
said
summer
soldier
sharing
smell
shiny
Shorewatch
story
special
sponser
snickered
school
scare

T

tricycle
trees
teepees
turkey
telephone
trick
took
table
thicker
tornado
together
team
today

U V

upon
use
vine

W

window
write
waves
why
wonderful
windy
which
woke
work
Williams
World War II
writing
while
watched
Wendy
witch
weak
wrote
worrying
whale
wife
whispered

Y

yelled
year

Z

zoo

WRITING TOOL KIT

WRITING TOOL KIT

Table of Contents

Writing Made Easy

Writing Made Easy

Writing Made Easy is a reference guide to help students use a variety of writing skills to achieve maximum student productivity. Each page specializes in a skill that will enrich a student's understanding of writing. *Writing Made Easy* shows the student how different components can be used to enrich his writing skills.

Each page in *Writing Made Easy* has important skills that are necessary in writing. By addressing each skill in *Writing Made Easy*, a student will understand how to improve his own style and include in his work the richness that will make him a success.

Scoring Written Work
(Teacher's Grading Tool)

I. Composes and organizes ideas:_____

    a. ____a clear beginning
    b. ____good sentence construction
    c. ____varied sentence structure and word choices
    d. ____rich details
    e. ____remains on topic
    f. ____figures of speech used
    (similes, metaphores, hyperbole, personification)

II. Uses CAPITALIZATION skills: _____

III. Uses punctuation skills:_____

IV. Uses correct grammar_____
    a. ____correct spelling

Reminders from your teacher:

_____

_____

_____

_____

Scoring My Written Work
(Student's Checklist)

Did I Use?

1. _____Complete sentences?
   (no fragments or run-on sentences)
2. _____Capitalization?
3. _____Punctuation?
   - a. _____end sentences using **.** **?** **!**
   - b. _____apostrophes
     apostrophes in contractions (**can't**)
     apostrophes in possessives
     boy's hat
     boys' hats
     men's hats
   - c. _____commas
     comma conjunction in compound sentences **, but** / **, and**
     comma in list (**soccer, tennis, and football**)
   - d. _____quotation marks
     quotation marks **"It's time to go,"** said Ted.

REMINDERS

DID I USE?

___thesaurus, spelling, indenting, left and right margins?
___use some compound sentences along with simple ones?
___begin my sentences in different and interesting ways?
___use a few transition words to move smoothly from one
   sentence to another? (However, At last)
___use an appositive? (John, my friend)
___a clear beginning and ending
___rich details
___remains on topic
___figures of speech used
   (similes, metaphors, hyperbole, personification)
___CAPITALIZATION skills
___use punctuation skills
___use correct grammar
___use correct spelling

Do I Have a Good Writing Style?

1.   How long are my sentences?

       (*need long and short one's…)

2.   How did I begin my sentences?

       *Variety (try to avoid "there is … "there are…)

3.   Some word no-no's:

       a lot   a little   things   very   much

4.   Have I used too many linking verbs? be

       was walking   is going   were leaving   am driving

5.   Are my compound sentences joined in the same way?

       *Use different methods: , and   semicolon;

6.   Did I use too many prepositional phrases?

       He went to town in a car to buy cokes for the party at the park.

Story Outline

I. Beginning Sentence:
    (who, what, where, when)

    _____

    _____

    _____

    _____

II. Body: (Main ideas in sequence)
    1._____

     _____

    2._____

     _____

    3._____

     _____

    4._____

     _____

    5._____

     _____

III. Ending Sentence: (How does your story end?)

    _____

    _____

    _____

    _____

Story Sequencing of Events

Introduction: **Who? What? Where? When? Why?**
Get information from prompts! One regular sentence, one feeling sentence,
one compound sentence

What happened first? (_____)_____
               (_____)_____
               (_____)_____
               (_____)_____
               (_____)_____

What happened next? (_____)_____
               (_____)_____
               (_____)_____
               (_____)_____
               (_____)_____

Then what happened (_____)_____
               (_____)_____
               (_____)_____
               (_____)_____
               (_____)_____

Later what happened? (_____)_____
               (_____)_____
               (_____)_____
               (_____)_____
               (_____)_____

Finally, what happened? (_____)_____
               (_____)_____
               (_____)_____
               (_____)_____
               (_____)_____

Conclusion: How did the story end?...
               (*I feel sentence and others.......)

Sentence Variety

Did I use some of these ways to begin my sentences?

____ subject first (**<u>The tiger</u>** woke up.)

____ adverb phrase (**<u>After the tiger woke up</u>**, he yawned.)

____ "verb" + ing (**<u>Seeing</u>** the tiger yawn was funny.)

____ transition words (**<u>However</u>**, the tiger didn't think it
                 was funny.)

____ introductory phrases
1. Last, but not least
2. Moving right along
3. In addition to
4. By the way
5. On the other hand
6. Along with
7. Instead of

____ Compound sentences (, conjunction , *and* , *but* , *or*)
       (We wanted to go, **<u>but</u>** it was raining too hard.)

____ Complex sentence

subordinating conjunction   **<u>Since</u> it is raining**, I can't go outside.

                 dependent clause   independent clause

Prefixes

Prefixes that mean NOT

1. dis = disallow
2. in = inactive
3. non = nonreversible
4. im = impolite
5. il = illegal
6. ir = irregular
7. un = unfair

Prefixes	Meanings	Examples
1. ex	out of, not, former	exclude
2. tele	far away	telescope
3. pre, fore	before	prepay, forewarn
4. sub	under	submarine
5. re	again	rewrite
6. trans	across	transcontinental
7. super	above, over	superhuman
8. mis	wrong	misinform
9. intra	within	intrastate
10. inter	between	international
11. con, com, co	together	connect, combine

NUMBER prefixes: semi = ½ = semicircle

1. uni = 1 = unify
2. bi = 2 = bicycle
3. tri = 3 = triangle
4. quad = 4 = quadruple
5. pent = 5 = pentagon
6. oct = 8 = octopus
7. dec = 10 = decade
8. cent = 100 = century

Write Your Own Story

Creative Writing Adventures

Storybook Writing

Students can write their own story using the storybook found on the following pages. The student has a title page, about the author page, outlines, picture story board, pages for story and illustrations.

Picture Story Summary

written and illustrated by

About the Author

Story Outlines

Story Outline in Spanish and English

Title:_____   Main Idea: _____
Titulo: Idea Principal:

People   **Scenes**   **Verbs**
Personajes   **Escenarios**   **Verbos**

Thoughts   **Problems**   **Solutions**
Ideas   **Problemas**   **Soluciones**

Feelings   **Character Trait**   **Items**
Emociones   **Caracteristica de Personajes** **Objectos**

Detailed Story Outline 3

Title:_____ : Main idea_____

4th - 8th grade

Scene:	**Scene:**
People:	People:
Verbs:	Verbs:
Thoughts:	Thoughts:
Problems:	Problems:
Solutions:	Solutions:
Feelings:	Feelings:
Items:	Items:
Scene:	**Scene:**
People:	People:
Verbs:	Verbs:
Thoughts:	Thoughts:
Problems:	Problems:
Solutions:	Solutions:
Feelings:	Feelings:
Items:	Items:

Title:_____

Main idea:_____

Defining Problems and Solutions

Problem   Solution

⇨

⇨

Determining Cause and Effect

Cause   Effect

⇨

⇨

Title / Main Idea

_____

- -

- -

- -

Picture Story Board

Picture Story Board

Title:_____

Picture Paragraph Outline

1st paragraph	2nd paragraph
3rd paragraph	**4th paragraph**
5th paragraph	**6th paragraph**
7th paragraph	**8th paragraph**
9th paragraph	**10th paragraph**

Title: _____

Main idea: _____

_____

_____

_____

_____

_____

_____

_____

_____

_____

_____

_____

_____

_____

_____

_____

_____

Creative
Writing
Adventures

Explanation
and
Overview
of
Outlines
and
Projects

Creative Writing Adventures
(Teach, Draw and Tell) TDT
(Research, Draw and Tell) RDT
PreK - 1st Grade

Objective: Students will learn to outline, illustrate, tell, write and edit a story. Students will learn to make comprehension questions with answers. Students will learn to research a topic to tell a story.

Procedure:

Teacher: (Teach, Draw and Tell) TDT
1. **Teacher:** Choose story. Teacher **teaches** background information about story. ex. Pirates: how they lived.
2. Teacher **draws** pictures of story on board.
3. Teacher **tells** story to class while showing illustrations of each scene in the story. (modeling)
4. Teacher explains how to make an outline and write questions and answers about the story.

Student: (Research, Draw and Tell) RDT
5. **Student** decides on topic,(ex.: jungles, Egyptians). Does **research**.
6. Student creates story focusing on main idea. Student makes outline.
7. Student **draws** scenes in story in sequence. (Picture Writing)
8. Student **tells** story to class from pictures. (Picture Storytelling)
10. Student makes comprehension questions about the story using picture answers.

Outcome: The student will produce a story with an outline and illustrations and tell the story to the class. He will write picture answers converted to questions about the story.

Materials: pencils, colored pencils or crayons

Two Types of Picture Writing

picture story

Picture Writing
{pictures and words}

Long ago there was a 🧍 who lived in an 🏠 .

He loved taking trips in his ⚓ . He kept his 〰️

at the ⚓ dock . One day he took his ⚓ to some

nearby 🏝️ islands .

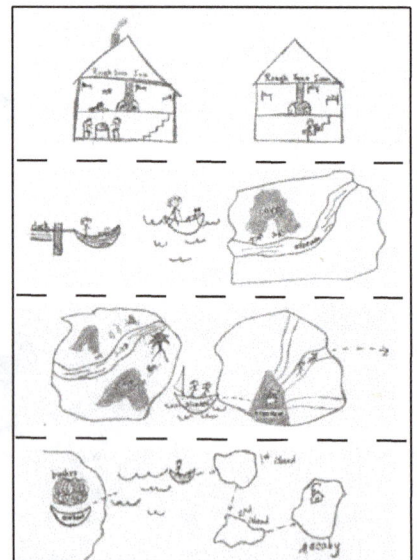

Adventures of the Rough Seas Inn

picture story summary

cover picture

picture story

picture outline

Title:_____ Main idea:_____

PreK - 1st grade

Example

people / animals	scenes / places
Tim Sam Sailor	Ando chimney
Crossbones Sandybones	caves island treasure
verbs / action words	thoughts / ideas
walking hiding	tent help
rowing sleeping	
finding	
turning swimming	bad monster sail fun

story written

One foggy morning two little Indians sneaked out of their teepee because they herd something. The girl name was Blue Bird the boys name was Eagle. When they went outside they herd this noise again. Blue Bird and Eagle always wanted to have an adventure so they went to go on one. They head it close to the forest so they went to look who made that sound. When they found the thing that was making that noise they couldn't believe it. It was a woodpecker.

questions & answers cards

Who is Crossbones?	Crossbones is a pirate.

Question on the front. **Answer** on the back. Cut out cards. Fold cards and glue together.

questions & answers

1.Q. Who are the main characters in the story?

A. The main characters are Eagle and Blue Bird.

2.Q. Where did the story took place?

A. The story took place in the forest.

3.Q. When did the story take place?

A. The story took place during a foggy winters day.

4.Q. Why did Blue Bird and Eagle sneak out of their teepee?

A. They sneaked out of their teepee because they heard something.

The Pirate Adventure

Defining Problems and Solutions

Problem		Solution
Poor	→	Found treasure
Needed a safe place to live	→	Found town of Macaby

Determining Cause and Effect

Cause		Effect
Tim's parents did not come home one night.	→	Tim walked the streets alone looking for his parents.
What caused Tim to take the pirate map?	→	Tim wanted to be wealthy.

Glossary
of
Literary
Terms

Literary Terms

Alphabetical Order: Words written in the same order as the alphabet by 1st letter.

Assessments: Tests or evaluations

Choral Reading: Teacher reads passage orally first then students read the same passage orally together.

Consonants: All letters of the alphabet except a, e, i, o, u.

Differentiated Instruction: Instruction that meets the student's individual needs.

Comprehension Questions: Questions about the story

Fluency: Oral reading the same way a person talks

Marker: White paper the width of the book used to cover words under the sentence being read.

Modeling: The teacher reads a long, detailed, and complex story using pictures drawn on the board. Each scene shows a problem with a solution. Modeling is used to show the student how to write a story including different people, scenes, verbs, items, thoughts, feelings, character traits, problems and solutions.

Model Story: An example of a complex story depicting people, scenes, verbs, items, thoughts, feelings, character traits, problems and solutions.

Non-writing program: A program that teaches without using words or letters. Example: Match words with pictures.

Literary Terms

Picture Answers: Pictures drawn to answer questions about the story.

Picture Comprehension Cards: Index cards written with a question on the front and the answer on the back referring to the story.

Picture Paragraphs: Author uses pictures to show the beginning of a new paragraph such as time, setting or new person talking.

Picture Paragraph Outline: Author divides white paper into ten parts. Each box is labeled Paragraph 1, Paragraph 2, etc. The author then draws a picture showing a new time, setting or person talking.

Picture Story: Story using pictures drawn in sequence.

Picture Storytelling: Author tells a story from pictures or scenes he has drawn in sequence.

Picture Story Board: Paper folded into fourths vertically. Author draws his story using pictures in sequence from left to right on each line.

Picture Story Outline: Author draws pictures to show people, scenes, items, feelings, problems and solutions found in the story.

Picture Story Library: Collection of Picture Story Books using hardback book covers. **(Lintor Make a Book Co.)**

Picture Story Summary: A summary of the story drawn using one picture.

Picture Writing: Author uses pictures or pictures with words to write his story.

Literary Terms

Possessive: showing ownership

TDT: Teach, Draw and Tell: <u>Teacher directed</u>: A method explaining the process used to teach a Creative Writing Adventures lesson.

First the teacher <u>teaches</u> the lesson. Next the teacher <u>draws</u> the story with pictures on the board. Finally the teacher <u>tells</u> the story using the model story.

RDT: Research, Draw and Tell: <u>Student directed</u>: A method explaining the student's role in creating his own Creative Writing Adventures story.

First the student <u>researches</u> the topic he wants to write. Next the student <u>draws</u> the outlines and story using pictures. Finally he <u>tells</u> his story to the class using his pictures of scenes drawn in sequence.

Sight Words: Words that are learned by sight, not by sound.

Story Outlines: Outlines are used to show different people, scenes, verbs, items, thoughts, character traits, problems and solutions. Each heading can be shown using pictures or words.

Story Papers: All work related to creating a story including story outline, story pictures, picture writing, written story, question and answer paper.

Synonyms: Words that have the same meaning.

Vowels: Letters a, e, i, o, u.

Word Recognition: recognizing printed words

Sand Prints Publishing Company

Figurative Language

1.Similes	Mom is as busy as a bee.	They're as crazy as a bee in a honey pot.	I sounded like a broken record.	She's as happy as a lark.	The tree swayed like silent dancers.
2.Metaphors	She's the apple of my eye.	He's a mountain of a man.	She is a rose without a thorn.	That car is a lemon.	He was a pillar of strength.
3.Personification	The angry truck growls at the stoplight.	A sportscar honks, "Hello!"	The stoplight winks its big green eye.	The soda machine swallowed my money and spit out a soda.	The happy bird sang love songs to the kids.
4. Idioms	Bury the hatch!	You have a feather in your cap.	Don't beat around the bush.	It's raining cats and dogs.	Let's go back to the drawing board.
5.Alliteration	My lazy lizard, Larkin, lives on lemonade and limes.	He fries frozen frogs on Friday.		On Tuesdays he tells tales to turtles.	
6.Hyperbole	Tom ran faster than a speeding bullet.	Mom told me a million times to clean my room.	He is so tall he can touch the stars.	Paul Bunyan carried a forest of trees under his arm.	
7.Onomatopoeia	slurp shuffle	clang bang	tweet hiss	meow creak	rustle squeak
8.Puns	A well is a deep subject.	A kindergarten teacher makes little things count.	The grizzly said, "I can't bear it anymore."	A teacher without students has no class.	To write with a broken pencil is pointless.
9.Analogies	teacher : student :: coach : player	nail : finger :: hair : head	gold : mine :: oil : well	bacon : eggs :: jelly : toast	father : mother :: son : daughter
10.Oxymorons	Stupid Genius	Happy Griever	Living Death	Roaring Silence	Cruel Kindness

Little Bug Adventure Books - Exciting learning books and DVD's for PreK - 8th grades

Little Bug Adventure Books

"We make Learning Fun and Easy!"

Three Little Bears Handwriting Program

Three Little Bears Handwriting Program instructional video for the class
$14.99
Format: DVD
Run Time: 18 minutes
Handwriting at its best! Teaches beginning manuscript handwriting. Use parts of the bears body to begin each letter. So much fun!

(K - 1st gr)

CREATIVE WRITING ADVENTURES: THE INDIAN ADVENTURE

Creative Writing Adventures: The Indian Adventure (DVD) instructional video for the class
$49.99
Format: DVD
Run Time: 18 minutes
Fun for every student! Creative Writing was never this exciting! Learn how to teach model stories, story outlines, story pictures, comprehension story games and so much more! Follows Blooms Taxonomy Guidelines for gifted students. (PreK - 8th gr.)

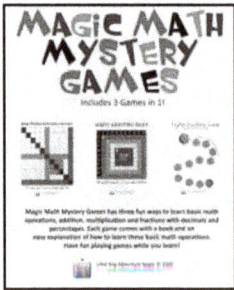

Magic Math Mystery Games
$19.99
Page Count: 30
Learn a quick way to complete the multiplication table. Also learn addition, subtraction, multiplication, division facts by playing games. Learn how to change fractions to decimals and percentages. (K - 5th gr)

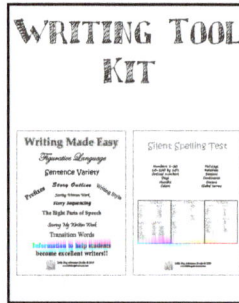

Writing Tool Kit
$12.99
Page Count: 40
Writing Tool Kit is a comprehensive collection of worksheets and activities that help students master writing skills. It also includes a silent spelling unit that teaches students how to spell basic word groups such as months, numbers, days of the week.
(2nd - 8th gr.)

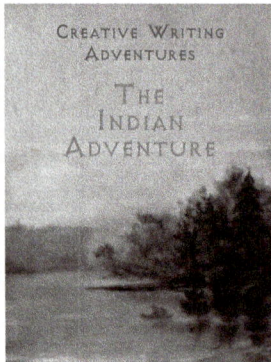

Creative Writing Adventures: The Indian Adventure
$16.99
Page Count:48
Teach your students how to write exciting adventure stories while teaching history and science. CWA uses model stories, story outlines, story pictures and story comprehension game. Follows Blooms Taxonomy Guidelines for gifted students. (PreK - 8th grade)

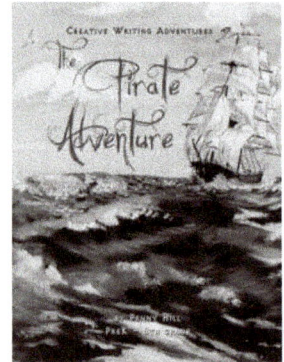

Creative Writing Adventures: The Castle Adventures
$16.99
Page Count: 44
Study medieval times with fairy tale castle adventures. Learn how to write sequel stories and include poetry and songs in your writing. CWA uses model stories, story outlines, story pictures and a story comprehension game. Follows Blooms Taxonomy Guidelines for gifted students. (PreK - 8th grade)

Creative Writing Adventures: The Pirate Adventure
$16.99
Page Count: 42
Explore pirate adventures that occur in 1492! CWA uses model stories, story outlines, story pictures and a story comprehension game. Follows Blooms Taxonomy Guidelines for gifted students.

(PreK - 8th grade)

More Quick and Easy Spelling, Reading and Writing Books

How to Make Letters Come Alive TE , Student Workbook and Activity Book

Book 1   introduces beginning consonants with six word families. grammar rules, dictation sentences and reading stories with comprehension questions. Writing Made Easy creative writing program.

Book 2 introduces beginning blends with word families [at, ip, ug, ed, and ob] grammar rules, dictation sentences and reading stories with comprehension questions.   Writing Made Easy creative writing program

Book 3 introduces ending blends, grammar rules, dictation sentences and reading stories with comprehension questions. Writing Made Easy creative writing program

Book 4 introduces diagraphs, dipthongs, grammar rules and dictation sentences and paragraphs. Writing Made Easy creative writing program.

Book 5 introduces word combinations using ion, ian, ture, etc. grammar rules and dictation sentences, paragraphs and stories. Writing Made Easy creative writing program.

Writing Tool Kit
Magic Math Mystery Games
Three Little Bears Handwriting Video

Creative Writing Adventures:
The Indian Adventure
The Castle Adventures
The Pirate Adventure

Adventures of the Rough Seas Inn
Story and Activity Book

Let Your Imagination Fly Away with You

Order books on-line at **www.littlebugadventures.com**

To see more exciting educational products visit
Little Bug Adventure Books at:
www.littlebugadventures.com

Sand Prints Publishing Company

www.ingramcontent.com/pod-product-compliance
Lightning Source LLC
Chambersburg PA
CBHW062104090426
42741CB00015B/3323